The lion and the rabbit

Retold by Beverley Randell
from an Aesop fable
Illustrated by John Boucher

"I am hungry," said a lion.
"I'll go and get
a rabbit to eat."

The lion got a rabbit.

The lion looked up.
"Here comes a big deer,"
he said.
"I'll go and get the deer.
This rabbit is too little."

And he let the rabbit go.

Away went the deer.

Away went the lion.

The deer ran and ran,
and the lion ran after it.
The deer ran fast . . .
and it got away!

The hungry lion came back to get the rabbit.

"My rabbit has gone!
It has **gone**!"
said the lion.

And he had to stay hungry.